CHORD JAMS
STRUM BOWING ETUDES BOOK 2

Cello

By Tracy Silverman

Music preparation by Tracy Silverman
Layout by Austin Gray   www.entireworld.us
Painting and Drawings by Rachel Kice   www.rachelkice.com
Photos by Matt Bell   www.mattbellviolinist.com

All compositions Copyright © 2020 by Tracy Silverman
All rights reserved.
ISBN 978-1-7348145-5-2

No part of this book may be reproduced or transmitted in any form or by any means, electronic or mechanical, including photocopying, recording, or by any information storage and retrieval systems without written permission from the author or publisher, except for the inclusion of brief quotations in a review.

Published by Silverman Musical Enterprises, LLC
Nashville, TN
info@tracysilverman.com | www.tracysilverman.com | www.strumbowing.com

Thank you thank you to Matt Bell of the electricviolinshop.com for all the photos in this book. Not only does he photograph electric violins, but he also plays them. Loud.

Follow him on Instagram @mattbellviolinist,
FB @mattbellviolinist,
Twitter @matt7738

Table of Contents

Section 1: Chord Jam Fundamentals — 1

   Chord Jam 1: Feelin' the Groove — 2

   Chord Jam 2: My Sweet Groove — 4

   Chord Jam 3: Dominant Strum — 7

   Chord Jam 4: Honeysuckle Groove — 9

   Chord Jam 5: Groovin' on the Circle — 11

   Chord Jam 6: Groovin' Further 'Round the Circle — 13

   Chord Jam 7: Strummin' Your Way Home — 15

Section 2: Chord Jams in Action — 19

   Chord Jam 8: Sly Strum — 21

   Chord Jam 9: Soul Groove — 23

   Chord Jam 10: Get Up and Strum — 26

   Chord Jam 11: Riff Rock — 31

   Chord Jam 12: Jammin' with the Geetars — 37

   Chord Jam 13: Cabbage Strum — 42

   Chord Jam 14: Drowsy Strum — 45

   Chord Jam 15: Jazz Blues in F — 48

   Chord Jam 16: The Long Way Home — 53

   Chord Jam 17: Strum Bossa — 58

   Chord Jam 18: Salsa Groove — 64

   Chord Jam 19: Get Groovy — 69

   Chord Jam 20: Groovy as Hell — 72

   Closing Words — 75

The Basics of
The Rhythm String Player

First of all, I am going to assume that you already understand the basics of Strum Bowing and are familiar with *The Strum Bowing Method*. **Chord Jams: Strum Bowing Etudes Book 2** is a progressive collection of etudes intended to accompany *The Rhythm String Player*, which picks up where *The Strum Bowing Method* left off. You can find info at StrumBowing.com

The Rhythm String Player is a way for string players to take Strum Bowing to the next level—to function like a rhythm guitar, either in a group or solo, able to accompany a singer or collaborate as a chordal instrument like the guitar.

Here are a few of the key concepts of playing rhythm on strings.

Playing Chords

The goal is to be able to accompany other musicians by playing rhythm. When we talk about backing someone up and playing chords, that means playing the bass notes as well as other chord tones and doing it in a rhythm that's appropriate to the style. It means reading a chord chart and making up a part.

Playing chords is a paradigm shift in how strings are played, because strings are taught and played generally as melodic instruments. We don't learn how to play chords like guitar players do. We are not considered a chordal instrument because our instruments aren't designed to play many strings at the same time.

But...

We can easily arpeggiate and essentially "fingerpick" chordal patterns using the rhythmic motor of Strum Bowing. Now that we have developed the ability to do a 3-D Strum, how do we apply it?

Many string players have very little understanding of harmony and how chords work. So, first let's break it down:

The Physics of Harmony

First of all, it often seems like a lot of theory and rules when you are new to it, but I find it helpful, especially as a string player, to remember that it's not arbitrary—there are simple physics in the harmonic series of overtones that cause things to sound the way they do, which we can categorize as Consonance and Dissonance. We just organize that into usable patterns, such as chords and scales. And it is not at all a dry and academic subject—for a musician, harmony is all about how music makes us feel. Songwriters and composers have always used the psychoacoustics of chord progressions to lead our emotions.

Consonance and Dissonance

- Consonance is when the harmonic series is stable. The overtones are aligned and resonate harmoniously, (frequencies tend to reinforce other frequencies.)

- Dissonance is when the harmonic series is unstable. There are overtones that are in conflict with other overtones, creating a sort of sonic war. It can sound like a beating at some frequencies or a kind of distortion, (an interaction of certain overtones known as wave interference which results in reinforcement and cancellation of certain frequencies.) It is by nature in conflict and therefore is active and seeks resolution.

The natural force of dissonance resolving to consonance is the engine that drives western harmony. This physical resolution of acoustical conflict has developed, in the hands of composers and musicians, into the musical cadence—a simple chord progression that gives a sense of resolution or returning to a home chord. The epitome of this is the V-I Cadence, also called the Dominant-Tonic Cadence. A close second is the IV-I Cadence, also called the Plagal or Amen Cadence.

This feeling of resolving by 5ths (V-I Cadence) is so strong that we can string them together as a series of resolutions, forming a Circle of 5ths. An example would be a ii-V-I Cadence or a vi-ii-V-I Cadence.

Reading a Chord Chart

The most important thing to know is that when we refer to chords, we use numbers in 2 different ways:

1. Chord numbers of the key, such as the V (five) chord in the key of C. We often use Roman numerals for this, following the classical tradition. More commonly we write the chord letter instead and refer to the number only when speaking about the form or chord function in the song, such as: "it goes to the IV chord here." (Except for the Nashville Number system, which uses the chord numbers as standard Aramaic numbers.)
2. Note numbers of a specific chord, such as the root, third, fifth, (1, 3, 5) of a C major chord. These numbers refer to the note of the scale and are typically used to signify an upper chord member, such as: a D7 chord, or a G7 flat13 chord.

It gets a little confusing when someone says to play a V7 chord, but you get used to it.

About Guide Notes:

Many of these Chord Jams have bars with chords of whole notes. These are intended to be Guide Notes, which are like cheat sheets, or reminders of the important chord tones.

About Tempos:

Most of the pieces deliberately have no tempo markings. This is because they can be useful at many different tempos, depending on your ability and approach to the etude—what you want to get out of it.

✗ = Ghost Note

╱ = Chop

Section 1: Chord Jam Fundamentals

Before we dig into jamming on tunes, we need to get some context. Because strings are taught and played primarily as melodic instruments, we don't think about chords much. Cello and Bass at least are familiar with bass notes and roots of chords, but upper string players are like sailors on a flat ocean of melody who are unaware of the chords and harmony swimming around beneath them.

This section serves two purposes: to teach some basic harmony to those who may not be familiar with it, and to do it on our string instruments, not on a piano or guitar. Let's make that connection between chords and our instruments at the earliest point in the process, for the very reason that chords are never taught on strings.

We will look at the idea of resolving by fifths, the V-I resolution, that is the driving force behind all western harmony—dominant chords, secondary dominants (ii-V-I) and the Circle of Fifths. This is the background you will need for Section 2, where we will dig into specific genres and how to be a rhythm player in different styles.

Chord Jam 1:
Feelin' the Groove
Dominants

The idea of this etude, and many like it in the book, is to play a simple chord progression using a 3-D Strum. The process is to take a given rhythmic structure, such as a groove, and take notes from chords (the Guide Notes) and mash them together.

What we're going to do here is to take the rhythm of the 3 Practice Grooves that we are already familiar with from the Strum Bowing Method Book and use the Guide Notes on the bottom staves as your notes.

For instance, you could take the note B flat and resolve it to an A 2 bars later like this:

Groove Prep
Chord Jam 1: Feelin' the Groove

Start by playing one note at a time, then see if you can play double stops. Try to get off the page and just play by ear. Feel free to change any of those Practice Groove rhythms—they're just a starting point.

Cello

1) Feelin' the Groove
Dominants

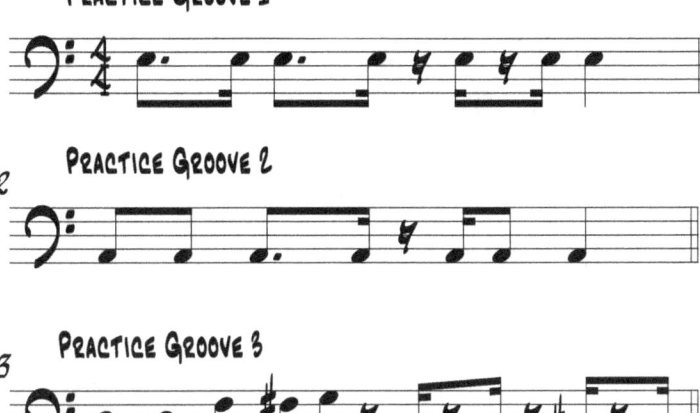

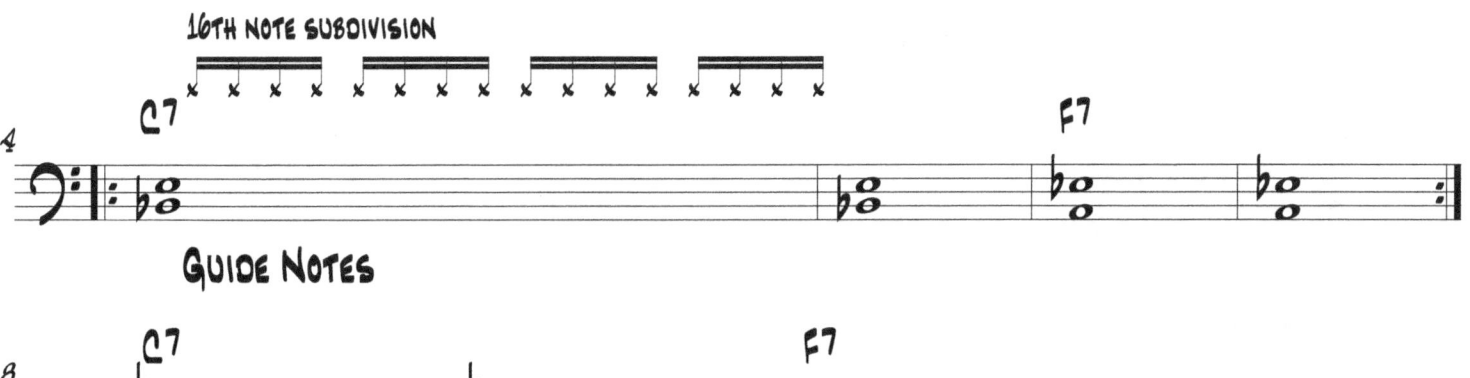

PLAY 3-D STRUMS USING THE GUIDE NOTES BELOW AND THE RHYTHMS OF PRACTICE GROOVES 1, 2 & 3 ABOVE

Chord Jam 2:
My Sweet Groove
The ii-V Progression

The most important notes of any chord are the 3rds and the 7ths, because they define the modality of the chord—whether it's major or minor or a dominant chord.

You can think of 3rds and 7ths as toggle switches with 2 positions: major 3rd or minor 3rd, major 7th or minor 7th.

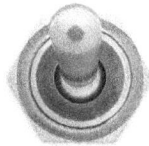 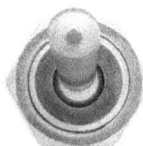

Major Chord: major 3rd, major 7th

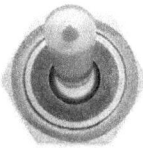 

Dominant Chord: major 3rd, minor 7th

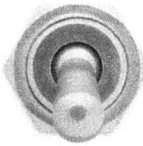 

Minor Chord: minor 3rd, minor 7th

Minor/Major Chord: minor 3rd, major 7th
(melodic minor scale)

Groove Prep
Chord Jam 2: My Sweet Groove

Play along with the track and be free with the groove. There are lots of possibilities.

Cello

2) My Sweet Groove
The II-V Progression

Guide Notes

Chord Jam 3:
Dominant Strum
Dominants with Extras

In a dominant chord, the 3rds and 7ths form a tritone.

When you move from dominant chord to dominant chord, that tritone moves down chromatically.

The upper chord tones 9, 11, 13 are the same as 2, 4, 6.

Groove Prep
Chord Jam 3: Dominant Strum

Once you get comfortable with double stops, see if you can add the 3rd note. You can break the 3-note chords into 2 double stops.

Cello

3) Dominant Strum
Dominants with Extras

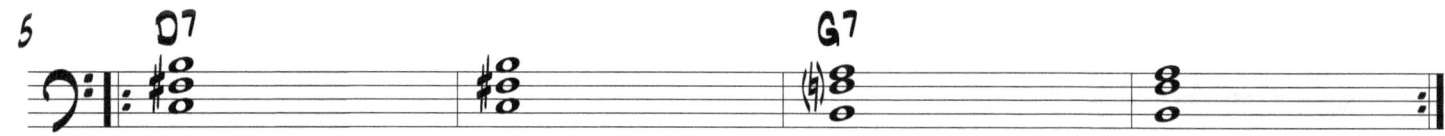
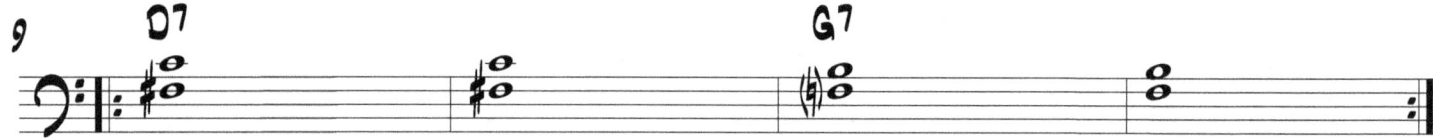

Chord Jam 3

Chord Jam 4:
Honeysuckle Groove
ii-V's with Toppings

Groove Prep
Chord Jam 4: Honeysuckle Groove

Free yourself to move while you play. Think of yourself as a drummer. Try to keep time with as many parts of your body as you can—nod your head, step from side to side, etc. Physicalize the groove.

Cello

4) Honeysuckle Groove
II-V's with Toppings

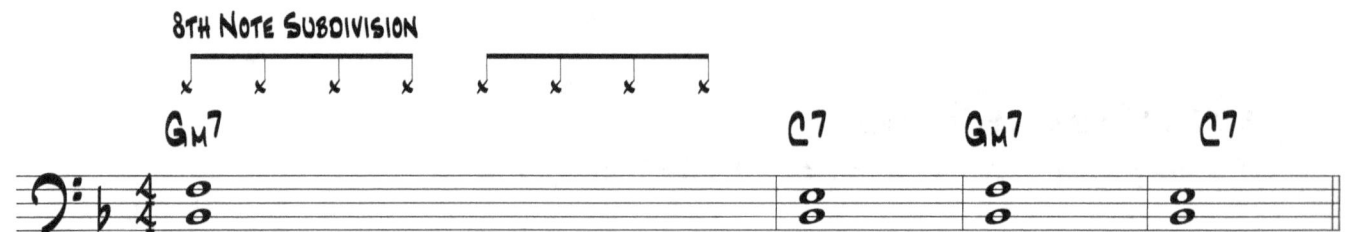
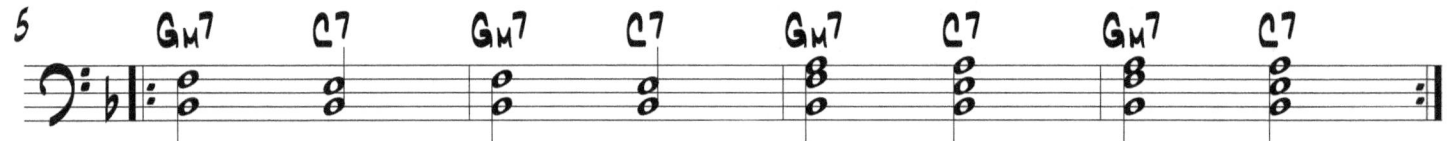

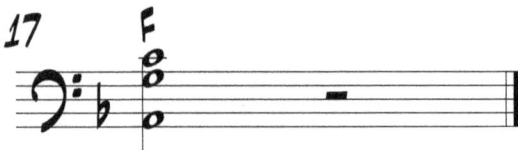

Chord Jam 5:
Groovin' on the Circle
Circle of Fifths

This 4-chord sequence demonstrates how the circle of fifths resolves from one chord to the next. It is also the same chords as the bridge of "I've got Rhythm" (otherwise known in bebop jazz as "Rhythm Changes," which is shorthand for: the chord changes to "I've Got Rhythm")

Groove Prep
Chord Jam 5: Groovin' on the Circle

Try playing with a swing feel. Then try it with a straight Latin feel. Focus on the descending inner melodies, either as single notes, which can start to feel a bit more melodic, or as double stops. Play with the idea of Percussive Bowing and the area where horizontal and vertical strokes mix.

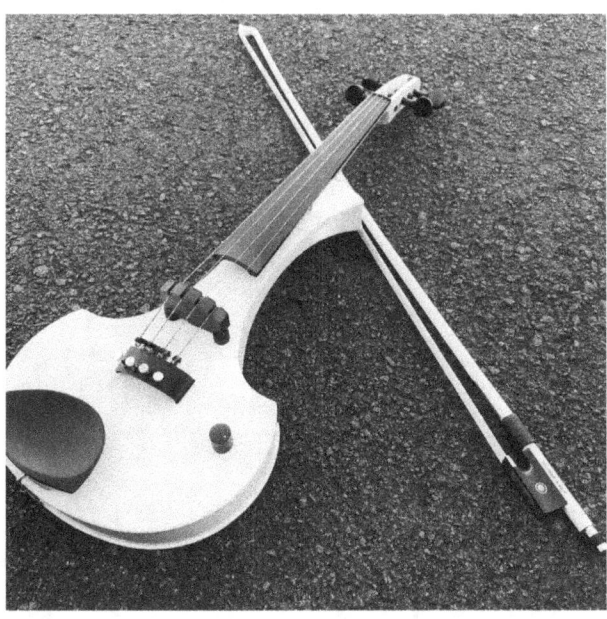

Cello

5) Groovin' on the Circle

Circle of Fifths

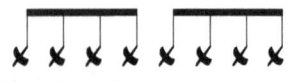
8th Note Subdivision

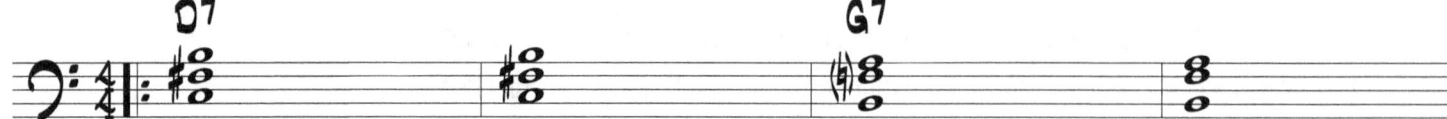
All 3 notes do not have to be played together

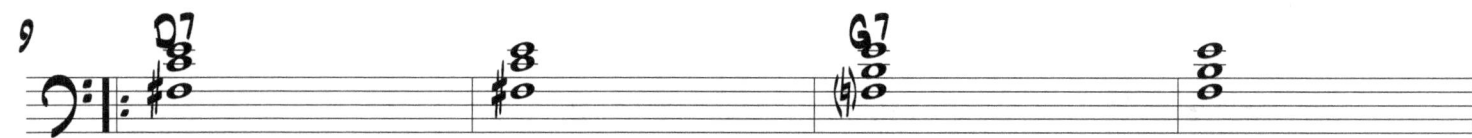

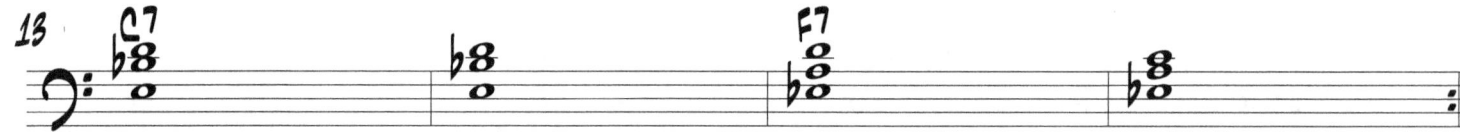

Chord Jam 6:
Groovin' Further 'Round the Circle
Circle of Fifths

This segment of the Circle of Fifths picks up where the last one left off. It's the same chords as "Sweet Georgia Brown." The trick here is to feel as comfortable with all those flat chords as possible. A lot of jazz tunes are in flat keys because they are better for horns.

Yes, these pieces have the Guide Notes written out, but all of these chord charts we've been playing have been getting you accustomed to the idea of looking at a chord symbol and improvising a rhythm part, something which is a long, long way from classical string pedagogy. Just sayin'.

Groove Prep
Chord Jam 6:
Groovin' Further 'Round the Circle

Again, focus on the descending melodic lines. It's always nice when you can combine rhythm playing with a sense of melodic motion as well. Playing this will also be getting you more and more accustomed to using 9ths and 13ths and to hearing those harmonies in your head.

Cello

6) Groovin' Further 'Round the Circle
Circle of Fifths

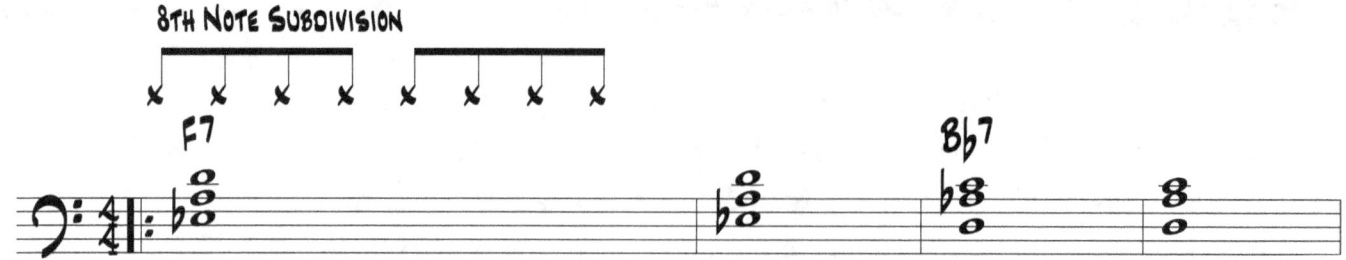

All 3 notes are not intended to be played together

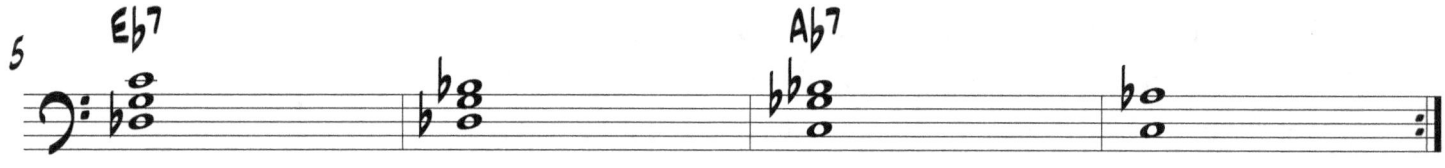

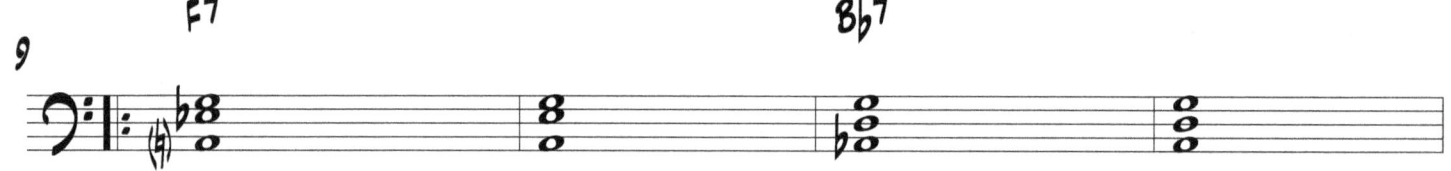

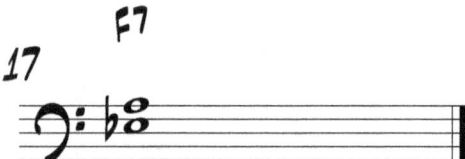

Chord Jam 7:
Strummin' Your Way Home
The ii-V-I Progression

The Circle of Fifths demonstrates how chords tend to resolve down by 5ths. But within any given key, we can use that force of resolutions by fifths to drive the harmony to the home key. The simplest version would be V-I. But we could resolve down a fifth to the V chord from its V, which would be the ii chord. Later we will add a longer series, such as the vi-ii-V-I and the iii-vi-ii-V-I, all of which are increasingly larger segments of the Circle of Fifths.

The important difference here from the string of dominant chords we have already looked at in Chord Jams 5 and 6 is that these chords are all diatonic to the home key, which just means that it uses only notes from the home key scale.

Use whatever groove you like. After this, we will be more specific about the rhythm of the groove, but for now, you can play any groove you like.

Chord Jams Bonus!

Where Chord Numbers Come From
The Diatonic Chords of the Major Scale

Groove Prep
Chord Jam 7: Strummin' Your Way Home

The goal with this one is to get your hand and ear accustomed to the 3 different keys so that you start to develop some automatic muscle memory. The ii-V-I progression, and just the ii-V part of it, are so ubiquitous in jazz, that it's important to develop this familiarity.

Cello

7) Strummin' Your Way Home

II-V-I Progression

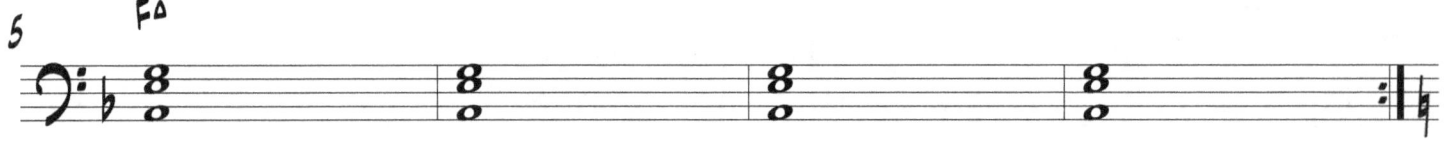
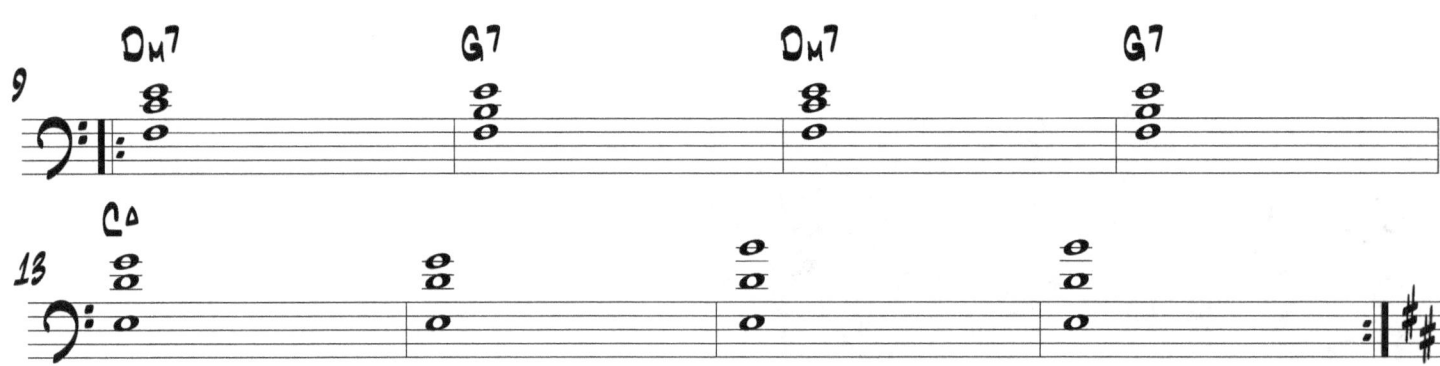

©2020 Tracy Silverman
From the Gut Music (ASCAP)

Section 2: Chord Jams in Action

In this section, we will look at the specific ways of playing rhythm in a few different styles.

- Funk
- Rock
- Folk
- Jazz
- Pop

Each one of these genres has its own way of thinking about grooves—Latin music is more ensemble oriented, with interlocking rhythms; Jazz is more harmonic, with the emphasis on voice leading (inner melodies), Rock can be chant-like, based on unison riffs.

I've assembled a couple of examples or generic architypes in each genre which will be the most useful to you. They have differing approaches, to give you the broadest possible palette of techniques to use as building blocks.

The intention is for you to work through them all and not to skip any. Even if you don't care for a style or ever intend to play it, there is something to be learned from it that you can't get any other way. Your goal should be to have a holistic approach to your instrument and a comfort level across a diverse variety of styles. Even if you don't generally play a particular style, you should understand it. And if you're a teacher, be able to teach it.

In all of these examples, we will look primarily at the rhythm guitar and bass parts. You can just work on the getting the rhythm guitar, since that is the main focus of this book. But I challenge you to try to also play the versions which are both bass and guitar. This makes these Jams substantially more difficult but makes you a much more useful player, able to be self-sufficient as a back-up player.

Chord Jam 8:
Sly Strum
Funk

Great rhythm players find a way to repeat a basic groove over and over, but always keep it fresh and never make you feel like it's getting stale or tired. It has endless energy and variety, even though it essentially keeps repeating. The trick is to not learn a part—a pattern of notes and rhythms—so much as to find a function—where and how you are emphasizing things.

Don't just learn a part and stick to it. Learn a function and play with it.

Groove Prep
Chord Jam 8: Sly Strum

Keep the notes as short as possible by dampening with your left hand. Stay between the middle and the frog for a percussive attack with the bow. Experiment with different notes for the rhythm guitar part in bars 5-8.

Chord Jam 9:
Soul Groove
Funk

Many funk tunes have a swing feel to the subdivision. Some instruments express that swing more than others. Generally, the drums will swing a little harder than the other instruments. So, it's good to be aware of the swing, but be careful that you don't overdo it.

Groove Prep
Chord Jam 9: Soul Groove

The horn riff at bar 13 is much more legato than any of the guitar or bass parts. It's tricky to switch back and forth between the two at bar 17, but try to stay as low in the bow as you can. At bar 21, be as free with the main guitar riff as you can—try different registers. Explore what you might do as a rhythm player in a jam to support someone who might be taking a solo over it.

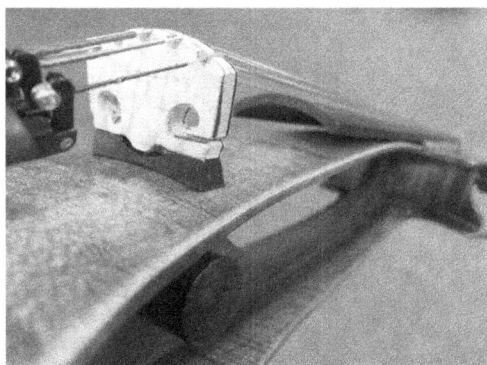

Cello

9) Soul Groove
Funk

Bridge

9) Soul Groove

Cello

Bass and Horns

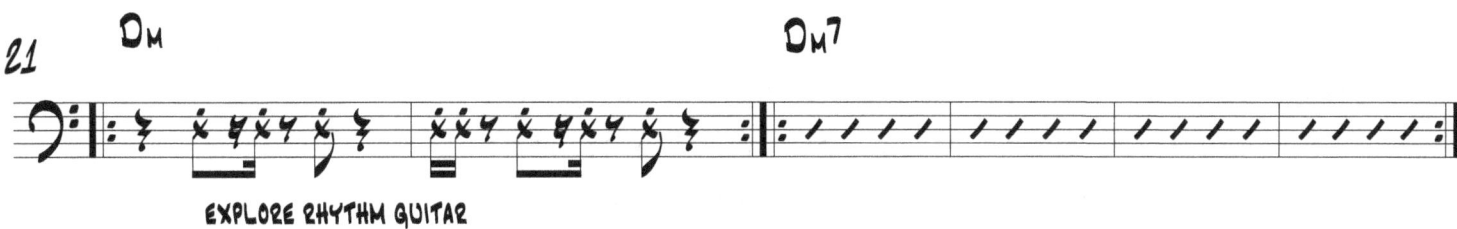

Explore Rhythm Guitar

©2020 Tracy Silverman
From the Gut Music (ASCAP)

Chord Jam 9

Chord Jam 10:
Get Up and Strum
Funk

The original key is not terribly string-friendly—E flat. It's good to get used to it, as it's a very common horn key, but it's much more idiomatic for strings down a half-step in D. It will probably demonstrate to you how much better you can groove in a friendly key, and how much better you can groove in general when things aren't too difficult.

It's necessary to practice difficult things in order to expand our technique and ability, but it's also important to play with ease, and that only happens when you play things which are easy for you, so don't ignore the simple fun of jamming on something really easy. In the world of rhythm playing, virtuosity is not such a virtue. Groove is everything. If it feels good, it is good.

Groove Prep
Chord Jam 10: Get Up and Strum

It's time to really focus on getting a dry, dampened articulation. It may surprise you at how much energy it takes to sustain that tight articulation. Playing rhythm is a very physical thing, which is why it's so important to use your whole body—not only to help you keep the tempo steady, but because you need to use the larger muscles in the back, legs and core to keep your arms from developing tension and tendonitis. Let your body help you: keep your arms, wrists and fingers as loose as you can, using the absolute minimum amount of tension, but be free about vigorously engaging the rest of your body. It's a kind of loose-arm groove dance.

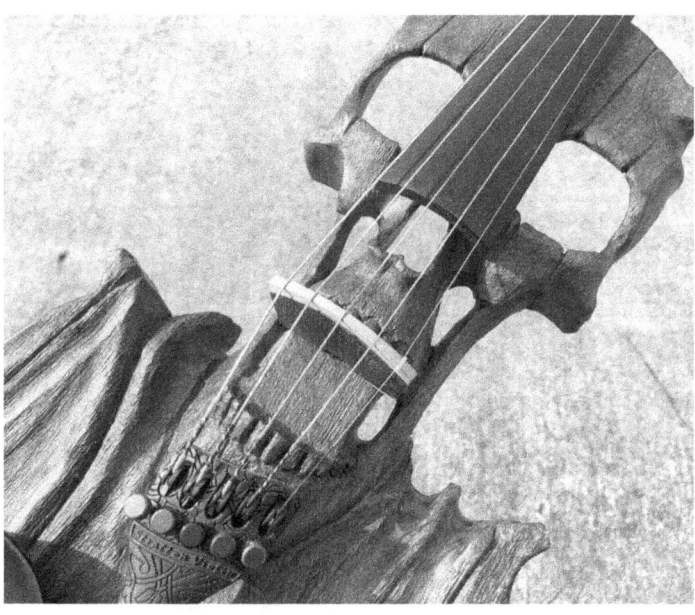

10) Get Up and Strum

Cello

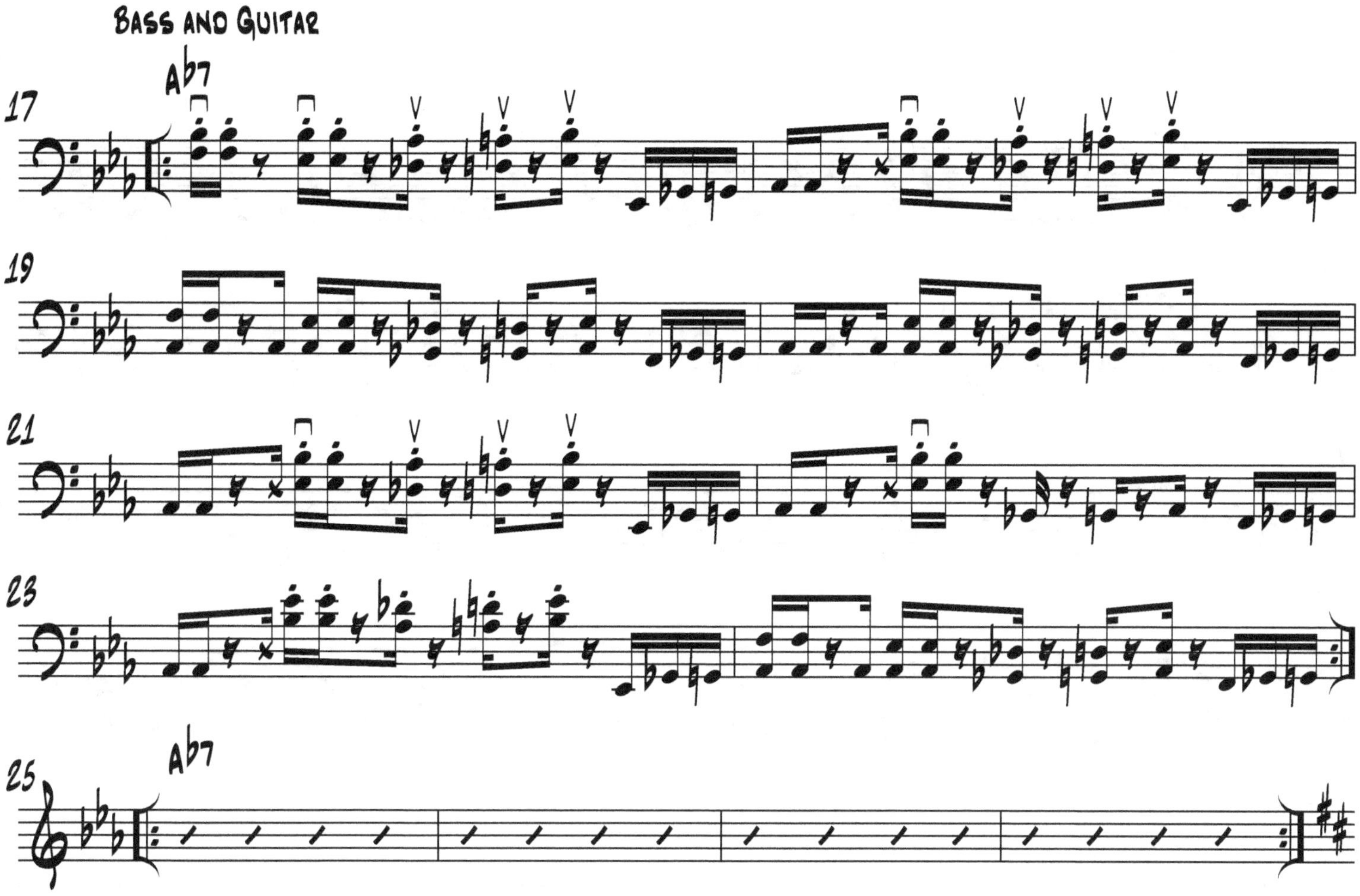

IN D

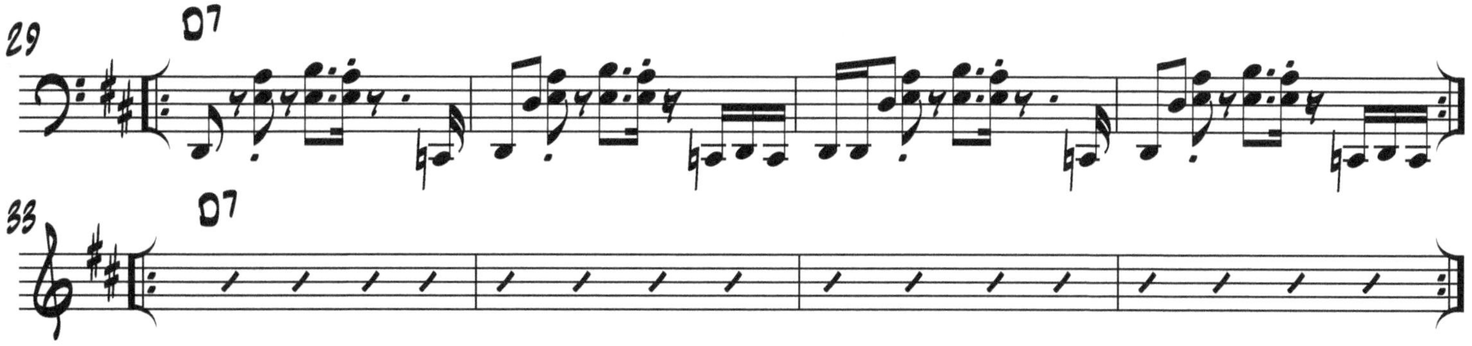

Chord Jam 11:
Riff Rock
Blues Scale in E

The Blues Scale is a slight modification of a simpler scale called the minor pentatonic scale, which is central to Rock and Blues.

On upper strings, you can play a one octave minor pentatonic starting with your first finger.

This simple frame or box can be transposed anywhere on the fingerboard.

The Blues Scale adds one note to the minor pentatonic, between the 4th and the 5th of the scale, but could be thought of as more of a gesture than a note—it is a bend or a push/pull of the note.

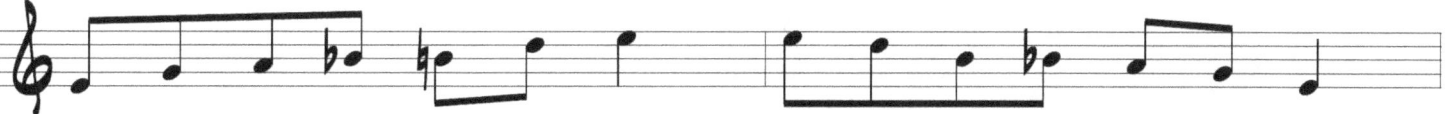

Because of the use of distortion, many rock tunes use power chords rather than more traditional chords. This only means that it has been reduced to its basics—the root and the fifth of the chord. All the additional 3rds and 7ths, not to mention the 9ths, 11ths and 13ths, have been eliminated. (Distortion makes all those intervals and dissonances too distorted to use.)

Instead, power chords (5ths) are often used as a rhythmic "chugging." Think Metallica. This is similar to rhythm guitar playing in other styles in that it is a rhythmic representation of the harmony. Other times, riffs (short melodic phrases) can be played in 5ths, which straddles the line between rhythm and melodic playing. Think "Smoke on the Water". For better intonation, try flattening your finger across the strings rather than approaching it in the more traditional classical way with the fingertip.

The minor pentatonic scale is central to Rock, so it's important to develop good muscle memory with it. Full Range One Position is the system I came up with to teach my students fluency with pentatonics. It encourages an even distribution of finger patterns so you don't get stuck in any muscle memory ruts.

Cello

Chord Jams Bonus!

Full Range-One Position
Minor Pentatonics

E Minor Pentatonic

F Minor Pentatonic

G Minor Pentatonic

Chord Jam 11

Full Range-One Position

Cello

A Minor Pentatonic

E♭ Minor Pentatonic

F# Minor Pentatonic

G# Minor Pentatonic

Groove Prep
Chord Jam 11: Riff Rock

First, get the E minor blues scale in your fingers. I used E because it's the key most use in rock due to the fact that guitars are tuned in E.

The riff at bar 9 bears a striking resemblance to a tune by Cream. Great minds.

At bar 29, make up your own riffs.

Cello

11) Riff Rock
Blues scale in E

Chord Jam 12:
Jammin' with the Geetars
Rock Blues in E

Learning how to jam on the blues may be the single most useful thing you can learn to get out of the classical box as a string player. It's so deeply rooted in our cultural ears that we don't have to learn it, just become more aware of it.

It's a short 12 bar form, consisting of 3 4-bar phrases, generally in an AAB pattern, lyrically. There is a strong home key which is defined by it's IV and V chords which resolve powerfully back to the main key.

It may be a little confusing, though, until you realize that there are several different versions of the blues. I've narrowed it down in this little chart to
- Delta Blues—Robert Johnson, Howling Wolf, etc
- Rock Blues— Chuck Berry , Led Zeppelin, etc
- Jazz Blues—Charlie Parker, John Coltrane, etc

Chord Jams Bonus!
Da Blues

Delta Blues

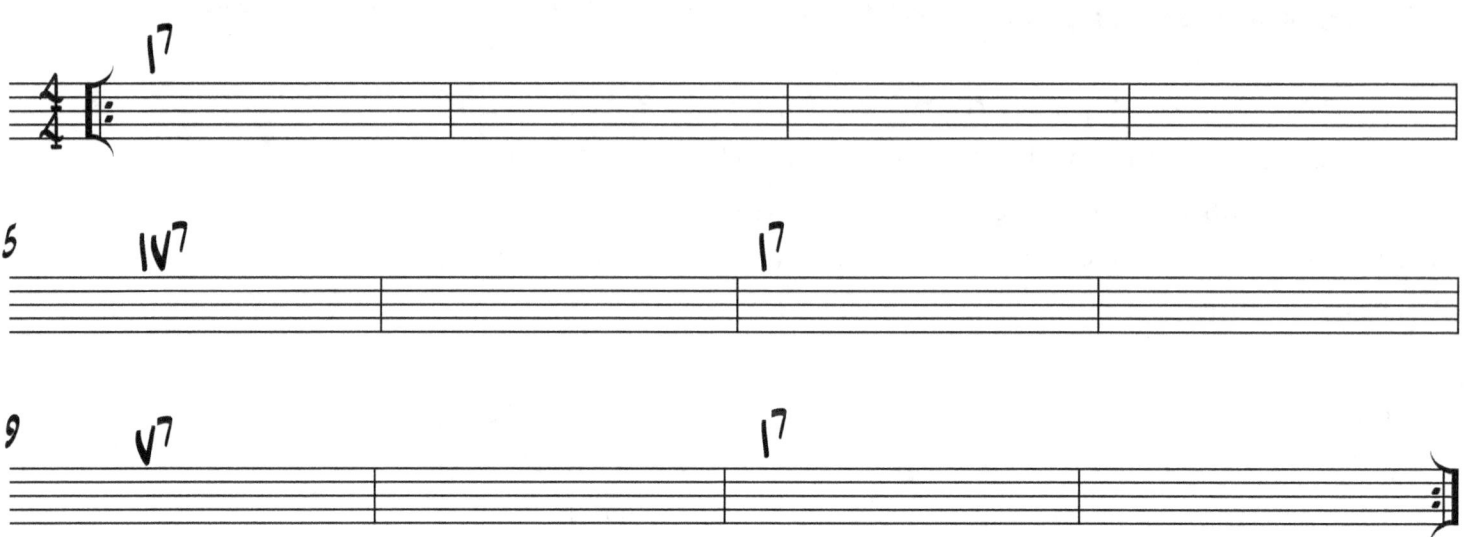

Rock Blues

Groove Prep
Chord Jam 12: Jammin' with the Geetars

You can play this with a straight feel or with a swing feel. If you swing the 8th's, we call it a blues shuffle or sometimes you might hear it referred to as a boogie rhythm, short for boogie-woogie, which was an early form of blues. If you straighten out the 8th's, it sounds more like early rock and roll like Chuck Berry. The harmony of the blues is so well understood by everyone that you barely have to imply the bass notes and the listener will fill in the rest.

Cello

12) Jammin' With the Geetars
Rock Blues in E

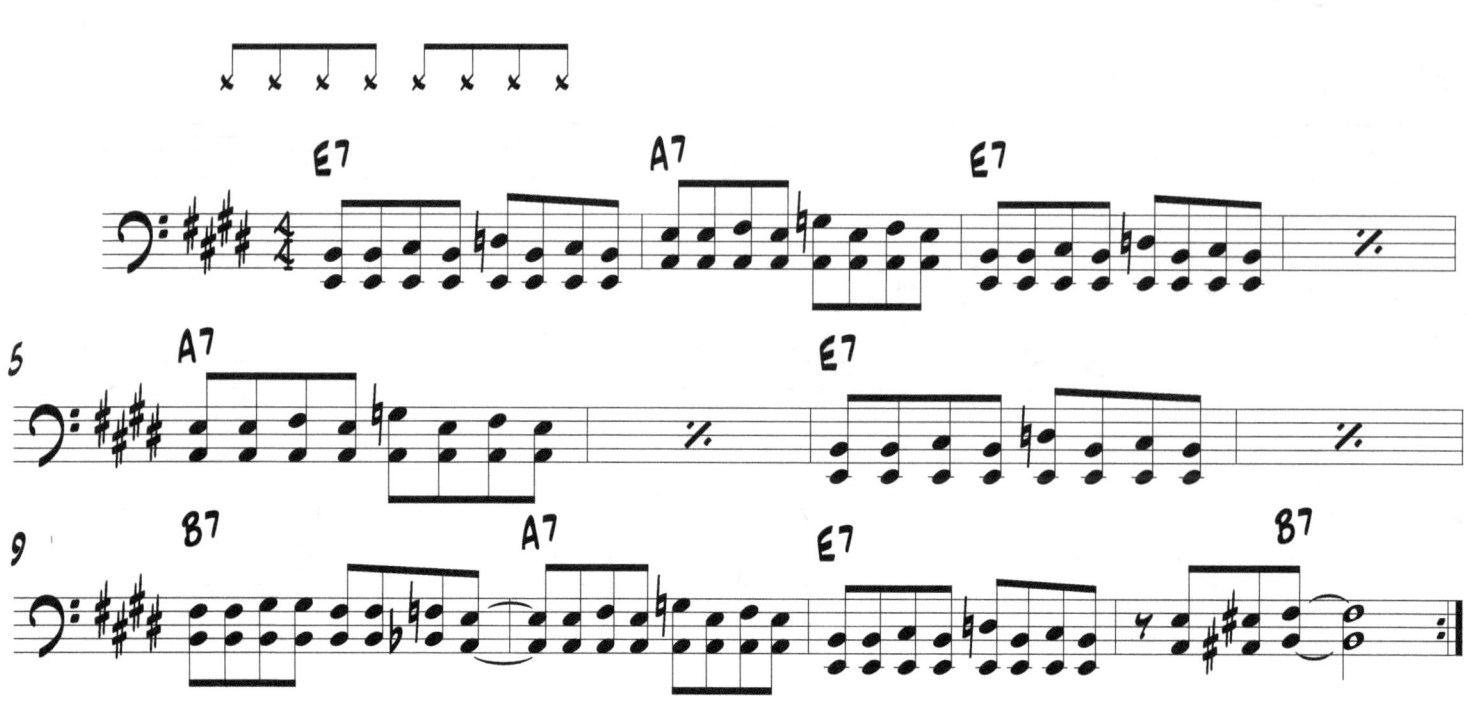

©2020 Tracy Silverman
From the Gut Music (ASCAP)

Chord Jam 13:
Cabbage Strum
Bluegrass

We are dealing with the same 3 chords—I, IV and V—as the blues, but this time the chord progression is a bit longer. This is a 16-bar tune which will sound very familiar.

One of the characteristics of a bluegrass rhythm section is that the bass will alternate between the root (the 1) and the 5 of whatever chord it is. In other words, if it's a C major chord, the bass will play alternate between C and the 5th member of the C major chord, G. If it's a D major chord, the bass will alternate between D and A, the 5th member of the D chord.

Groove Prep
Chord Jam 13: Cabbage Strum

Try to really think chordally. Without a clearly defined melody or riff, your job is to create a functioning harmonic groove that's appropriate to a bluegrass feel. You could sprinkle in some chops on some of the backbeats. As the piece progresses, I add more and more of the 8th note subdivisions. For the last 16 bars, as always, improvise your own version. Try to add some 8th note subdivisions in there occasionally, (simple scales always work well.) You will have to replace a few bass notes to do this, but then you can jump right back to the bass part to keep the sense of the bass line intact.

Chord Jam 14:
Drowsy Strum
Celtic

This is based on the well-known Irish tune, Drowsy Maggie. The tune is based on the Dorian mode, (the ii chord,) which is a minor key. As in bluegrass (and as you will soon see, also in most Latin styles,) the bass alternates between the root and the 5 of the chord.

Groove Prep
Chord Jam 14: Drowsy Strum

It's very helpful to sing the bass notes while you play, to really ground your ear and make sure that you are hearing the chords in your head as you are playing them. The bass note is something upper string players are not accustomed to focusing on.

Use short guitar-like bowstrokes that are not too melodic when playing rhythm. Melodic lines tend to be more present and sound more like a solo instrument, so when you are playing rhythm, it's better to be more supportive and less soloistic.

Cello

14) Drowsy Strum
Celtic

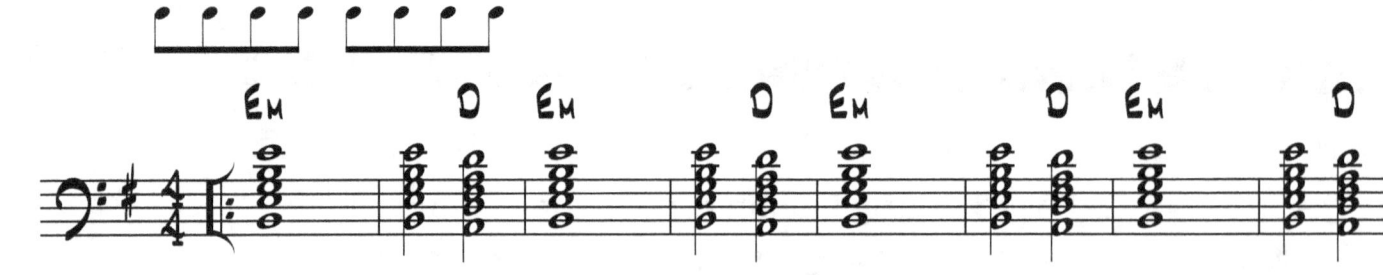
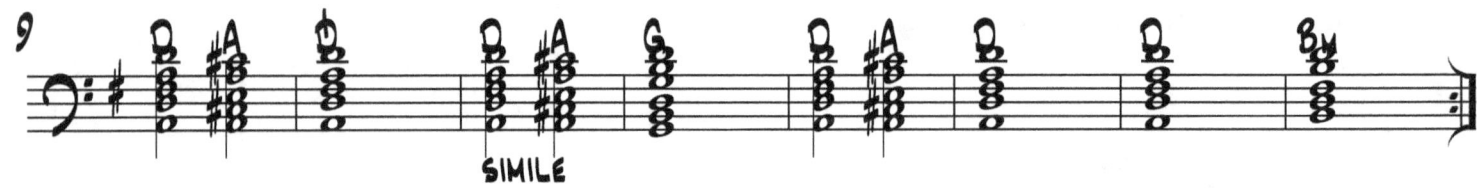

©2020 Tracy Silverman
From the Gut Music (ASCAP)

Chord Jam 15: Jazz Blues in F

First, jazz can be a little intimidating, so do yourself a favor and listen to a bunch of recordings of jazz blues—Charlie Parker, Coltrane, Miles Davis, Oscar Peterson, etc —and just get familiar with the sound of it. Try to sing the bass lines so you can hear the simplicity of the blues through the various harmonic additions. Like a foreign language, the more you hear it, the less foreign it sounds.

There's a lot to absorb here, so if parts of it are a little too advanced right now, come back to it soon and you may be surprised that it has become easier.

One of the main differences between the Jazz Blues and the Rock Blues is that in the last 4 bar phrase, instead of V-IV-I it's ii-V-I, which is more typical of jazz.

Rhythm guitar playing in jazz consists mostly of something we call "comping" which is short for accompanying. Comping is an art in itself. The idea of comping is to support the harmony in an understated way, with a minimum of strategically placed chords. Most jazz comping lines should be quite sparse and rhythmically as angular and unpredictable as possible.

Groove Prep
Chord Jam 15: Jazz Blues in F

There are lots of possibilities here for guide notes. I have 3 different versions of guide notes you can pull from. They get successively jazzier as they go, including more of the upper chord tones and chromatic harmony that increases the sense of tension, which in turn increases the power of the resolution.

Try to make interesting melodic lines by connecting guide notes from one chord to the next. You should start with just a single note and then try to add a second note. Then you can try to add more of the guide note tones by breaking or arpeggiating. You can make this as simple or as complex as you like.

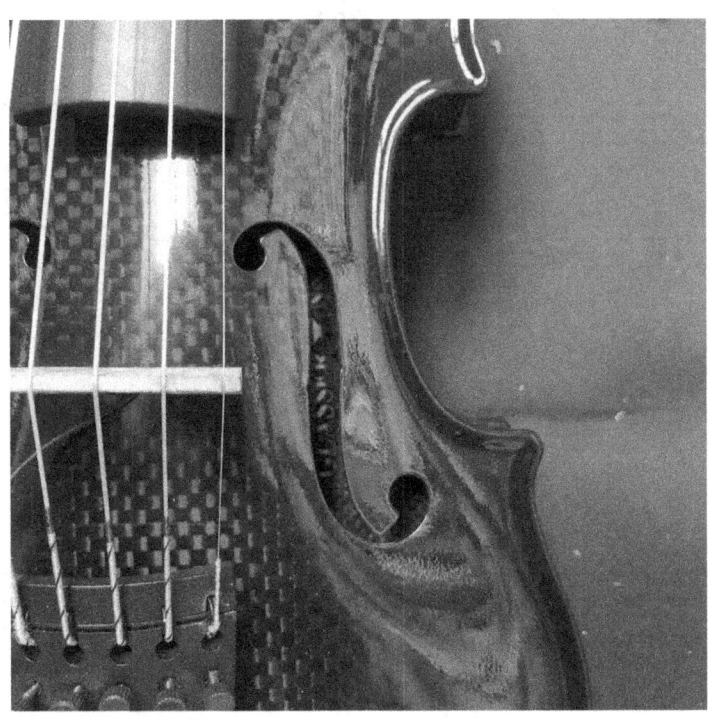

Chord Jam 16:
The Long Way Home
iii-VI-ii-V-I

Earlier in Chord Jam 7, "Strummin' Your Way Home," we played with the ii-V-I progression. This takes that a step further. We can precede the ii chord by its V chord, (sometimes called a secondary dominant or the V of the ii,) which would be the VI chord. And we can precede the VI chord by its V, which would be the iii chord. So the iii-VI-ii-V-I is a string of resolutions by 5ths (part of the Circle of Fifths) which lands on the 1 chord.

It's a very familiar sound. It's also the chord changes used in "I Got Rhythm," (Rhythm Changes.)

This is a good time to share with you an important insight into how to play chords, something I think of as the corollary to the bar chord on the guitar—a basic chord shape that you can transpose anywhere on the fingerboard.

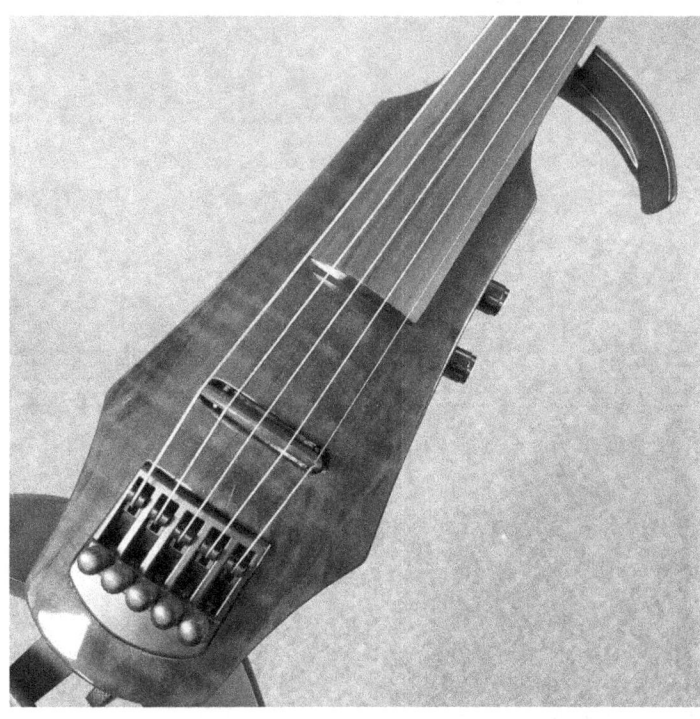

Chord Jams Bonus!
The 3-Finger Chord Shape

3 Modalities: Minor, Dominant, Major

The 3-Finger Shape in a II-V-I Pattern

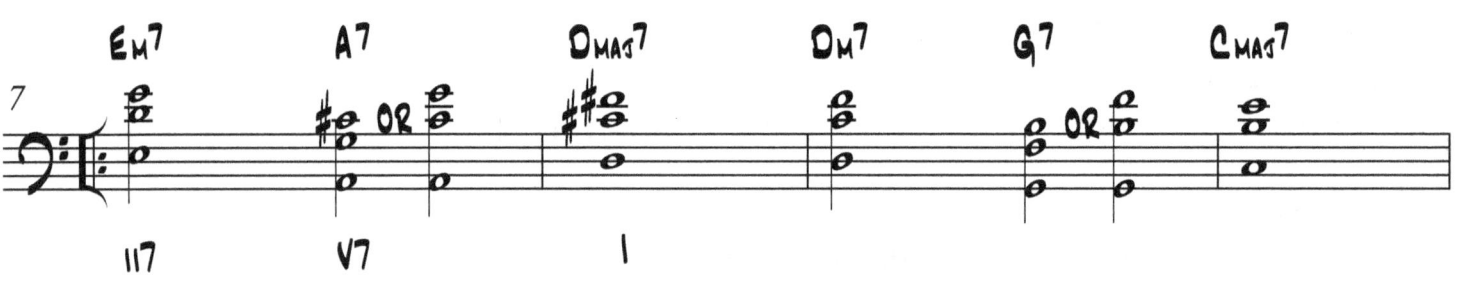

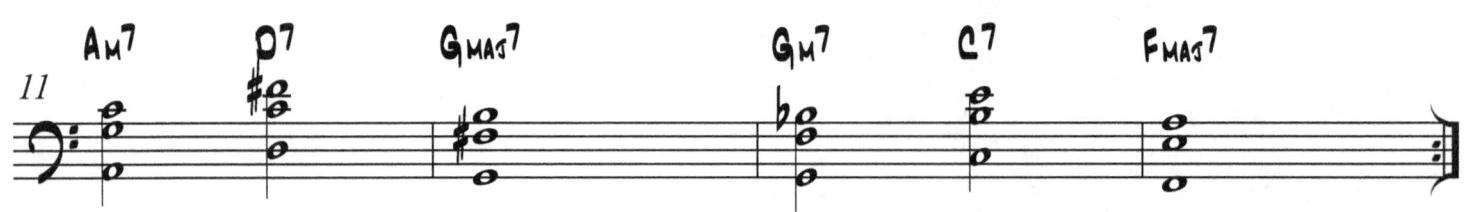

Groove Prep
Chord Jam 16: The Long Way Home

As in #15, the guide notes get progressively jazzier and I've given you an idea of the comping by itself as if you were playing with a bass player (bar 25) and also how you can juggle the bass line at the same time (bar 41.)

Again, you will help yourself by singing the bass notes.

Cello

16) The Long Way Home
III-VI-II-V-I in C

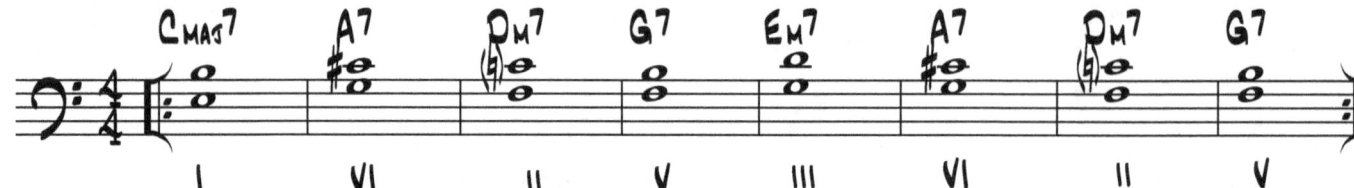

©2020 Tracy Silverman
From the Gut Music (ASCAP)

Chord Jam 17:
Strum Bossa
Latin

The first rule about Latin grooves is that they have straight 8th's as opposed to swung 8th's. The Bossa Nova rhythm developed in the 60's in Brazil and is a kind of cool jazz version of Samba, which is an up-tempo Brazilian dance groove played most notably during Carnival.

As with Bluegrass and Celtic music, the bass will alternate between the root and the 5 on the strong beats, and the guitar rhythm includes a lot of gentle syncopation.

This tune, based on "The Girl from Ipanema," introduces you to the Tritone Substitution. This simply means substituting the all-important dominant chord with its tritone. So instead of the V in a ii-V-I, it becomes a flat ii: ii-!ii-I

Chord Jams Bonus!
Tritone Substitution

Groove Prep
Chord Jam 17: Strum Bossa

Play through the tune with each of the 5 rhythms shown at the beginning. This style works well in the middle of the bow with a breathy, on-the-string kind of stroke.

At bar 27, I give you an example of how you could realize it with the 2nd rhythm. At bar 35, I'm using the 4th rhythm. Then at 51, we juggle both the bass line and the guitar part. This is typically all done on acoustic guitar with a finger-picked kind of style, the thumb alternating bass notes while the fingers pluck the treble notes. A good example of this style is Joao Gilberto.

Cello

Strum Bossa

Chord Jam 17

Chord Jam 18:
Salsa Groove
Latin

This is a style which originated in Cuba. All the percussion revolves around a central rhythm key, called the Clave, which is the rhythm in bars 1 and 3. One is just a reverse of the other. On top of this, many other percussion instruments and rhythms can be layered, such as the next 3 rhythm examples.

Another important characteristic of this style is the Montuno. This is how the rhythm part is expressed in this style. The rhythm part might be comping in jazz, or the finger-picking guitar syncopations in Bossa Nova, or chugging power chords in Rock. In this style, it is the Montuno, which is usually played on the piano, often in octaves. A Montuno is a highly syncopated arpeggiated chord figure and often has a chromatic moving line as part of it.

The chord progression is just a typical 4-chord vamp in a minor key that you might find in many salsa tunes.

Groove Prep
Chord Jam 18: Salsa Groove

First play through the calve and other rhythms using notes from the guide tones. Then get comfortable with the Montunos at bars 19 and 27.

The bass line is a bit more complex than the simple alternating style we've seen and has a very distinctive syncopation or "push" of its own on the 4th beat.

Putting the Montuno together with the bass line is not easy. I would recommend you slow it way down and practice with a metronome, getting faster one notch at a time. Tried and true.

Cello — Salsa Groove

Chord Jam 19:
Get Groovy

This song is a great example of rhythm guitar playing (by Niles Rogers.) The main guitar part is at bar 15, but it makes a good vehicle for practice, so I broke it down and isolated the rhythm of the guitar at bar 9 (a simplified version of it is at bar 10 so you can clearly see the underlying hemiola) and the Guide Notes at bar 11. So, you can use the same format of plugging guide notes into the given rhythm and explore other possibilities.

Notice how the guitar part is repetitious but always effective because it is constantly changing in subtle ways that don't disturb the groove, but keep it fresh.

Groove Prep
Chord Jam 19: Get Groovy

The rhythmic device that powers the tune is the tension and playfulness between the very straight up and down march-like bass part and the very syncopated cross rhythm in the guitar. Once you get both of these feels down separately, try and combine them as I do in bar 19. It's a compromise, for sure, but good practice. Play along with the record.

19) Get Groovy

Cello

Get Groovy

Cello

Chord Jam 19

Chord Jam 20:
Groovy as Hell

The challenge for strings is that we can't just copy our part from the record like a drummer or a bass player can. For one thing, we are playing string instruments which are never included in a rhythm section because the sound of strings is too classical. Secondly, we are trying to create a representation of drums, bass, guitars and keyboards on these old-fashioned instruments, not just typical string parts.

So while we are learning these tunes and these riffs, don't expect that what you play has to sound just like the record. It won't. It's something new. It's not a drum, it's a violin being played like a drum. It's not a guitar, it's a cello being played like a guitar.

Our goal is to capture the rhythmic groove of a tune and interpret it on our instruments in a way that is both authentic to the style and idiomatic to string instruments. I refer to this as post-classical string playing.

Groove Prep
Chord Jam 20: Groovy as Hell

Keep the articulation crisp by dampening with your left hand. Lift your fingers almost off the strings immediately after playing notes to mute them. Try to capture the subtle swing feel. It's a tricky shift of gears to go from the heavy rhythmic drive of the groove to the melodic vocal part in bars 12 and 14. Don't allow the groove to be disturbed in any way when you do this. Play along with the record or with a metronome. Better to leave out a note or two than to alter the beat in any way to accommodate the difficulty. This is always true for playing grooves.

The steadiness of the groove is sacrosanct. You don't get to slow down when it's hard or speed up when it's easy. There is no rubato of any kind when playing a groove. Its power comes from the inevitability of the pulse. A groove represents eternity.

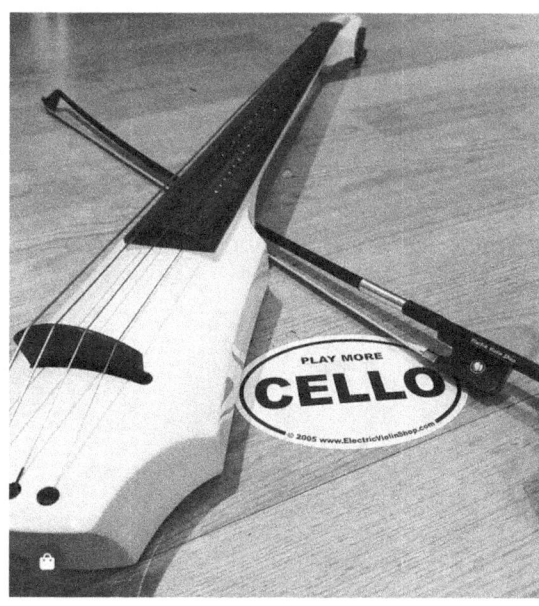

Cello

20) Groovy as Hell

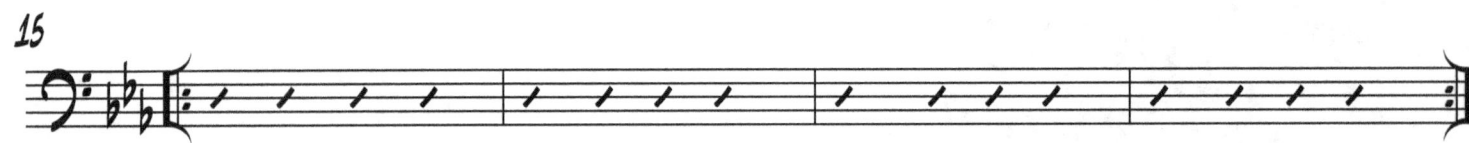

©2020 Tracy Silverman
From the Gut Music (ASCAP)

Chord Jam 20

Closing Words

In your quest to be a rhythm player, one important skill is to be able to keep a tempo steady. Engaging your body is key to this, as I've written about earlier. But you can also think of it as a sense of balance that comes from being perfectly comfortable or at ease with what you are playing—you aren't slowing down, you aren't speeding up, you are just right where you are.

This can happen at many different tempos, and the key is to find that balance and ease that allows you to stay exactly where you are. It's like you are planted into the earth and can't be moved.

Keep in mind that rhythm playing is not about virtuosity, it's about groove. Sometimes very simple things can feel great. To a string player, accustomed to a life of struggle just to make pleasing sounds, it may seem too simple. It's not. Sometimes it doesn't take much. At other times, it needs to sound simple but may actually be really awkward at first to pull off on a string instrument. It may take a while til there's any sense of ease and comfort.

But give yourself some time to repeat these grooves over and over. Take all your newly-gained ease and comfort and this new awareness of groove steadiness and revisit some of the earlier Chord Jams. Customize them to feel more comfortable. This is one of the wonderful parts of playing in a non-classical context. You get to play whatever feels good to you, to make it your own in a way you may never have gotten to do before with classical music, where your job is primarily to play what's on a page. Explore this new freedom! The only rule is that the groove reigns supreme.

If it feels good, it is good. And if it doesn't, keep groovin' til it does.

photo: Eric England

For play-along tracks for every etude in this book, and for all things Strum Bowing related, please visit **Strumbowing.com**

If you'd like to work on these etudes with me, please visit my online courses: **strum-bowing-groove-academy.teachable.com**

For information about workshops/clinics/residencies, teacher training, online lessons, speaking engagements or performances, you can reach me at **info@tracysilverman.com**

Please visit me at **tracysilverman.com** where you can sign up for my newsletter, **The Scuttlebutt**.

Follow me at:
Spotify: fanlink.to/spotify-TS
Instagram: @tracysilverman
Facebook: TracySilvermanMusic
Twitter: @tracysilverman
YouTube: youtube.com/tracysilverman

Grooooooooooove on

www.ingramcontent.com/pod-product-compliance
Lightning Source LLC
Chambersburg PA
CBHW081158070526
44583CB00021B/2891